Going Wild

HELPING NATURE THRIVE IN CITIES

MICHELLE MULDER

ORCA BOOK PUBLISHERS

Library and Archives Canada Cataloguing in Publication

Mulder, Michelle, 1976–, author
Going wild: helping nature thrive in cities / Michelle Mulder.
(Orca footprints)

Issued in print and electronic formats.
ISBN 978-1-4598-1287-1 (hardcover).—ISBN 978-1-4598-1288-8 (pdf).—
ISBN 978-1-4598-1289-5 (epub)

1. Urban vegetation management—Juvenile literature. 2. Vegetation management--Environmental aspects—Juvenile literature. 3. Urban plants—Juvenile literature. 4. Urban animals—Juvenile literature.
I. Title. II. Series: Orca footprints

SB472.7.M85 2018   j712   C2017-904558-x
C2017-904559-8

First published in the United States, 2018
Library of Congress Control Number: 2017949711

Summary: Part of the nonfiction Footprints series for middle readers, illustrated with many color photographs. Readers will find out what urban rewilding is and how it can make our lives (and our planet) safer and healthier.

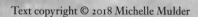

Orca Book Publishers is dedicated to preserving the environment and has printed this book on Forest Stewardship Council® certified paper.

Orca Book Publishers gratefully acknowledges the support for its publishing programs provided by the following agencies: the Government of Canada through the Canada Book Fund and the Canada Council for the Arts, and the Province of British Columbia through the BC Arts Council and the Book Publishing Tax Credit.

Front cover images: iStock.com
Back cover images (top left to right): Erin Clarke, Dreamstime.com, Dreamstime.com
(bottom left to right): iStock.com, iStock.com, Wikipedia

Edited by Sarah N. Harvey

ORCA BOOK PUBLISHERS
www.orcabook.com

Printed and bound in Canada.

21 20 19 18 • 4 3 2 1

For Alvera and Henry

Did you know that spending time outside is both fun and good for your health?
JOHN RUSSELL

Contents

CHAPTER THREE:
LIFE IN THE CITY

CHAPTER FOUR:
WILDLIFE WELCOME

Introduction

Our family loves a day at the beach, even when it's cold enough for winter jackets!
MICHELLE MULDER

Have you ever run from a bear or a lion? If you're one of the world's 3.5-billion city dwellers, you're probably safe from big wild animals. After all, humans have spent thousands of years keeping unwanted creatures out of our cities. But did you know that many cities are reshaping themselves now to let more wild nature *in*?

I'm a city dweller myself, but I never expected to be. I imagined becoming a park ranger and living in semi-wilderness. Then I met my husband, who loves cities like his hometown of Buenos Aires, Argentina, which has thirteen million people. Together, we started searching for a place that would be comfortable for both of us, and we chose a small city on Canada's west coast. Here we can visit museums, art galleries and theaters just as easily as we can spot woodpeckers, barred owls, otters and deer.

I used to think this city/nature balance was only possible in a small place, but lately I've been reading about big cities making space for wild nature too. In Seoul, South Korea, city workers ripped out a highway to release the stream trapped beneath. In Adelaide, Australia, kids helped plant three million *native* trees, creating new homes for local wildlife. Around the world, adults and kids are breaking up pavement and *rewilding* our cities for both human health and the health of the planet. How? Grab a shovel and some binoculars, and come find out!

Looking out my living room window a few years ago, I learned that raccoons love cherries as much as I do. TIM BRAY

Making Tracks

While I was writing this book, I tried to spend at least half an hour a day enjoying nature. My daughter and I cloud-gazed in a meadow, listened to red-winged blackbirds sing in a bog, poked around beaches and watched pods of orcas frolic in the waves. This meadow in our local park, which turns purple with camas flowers in May, was one of our very favorite spots.

The flower-filled field at our local park is perfect for cloud gazing. MICHELLE MULDER

CHAPTER ONE

Paving the Way

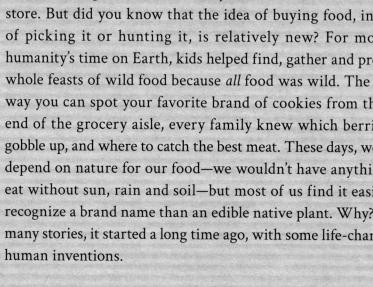

MMM, WILD BREAKFAST

Have you ever eaten something wild? A juicy blackberry maybe? Or a fish you caught yourself? It's not every day we eat something that came directly from the wild instead of a store. But did you know that the idea of buying food, instead of picking it or hunting it, is relatively new? For most of humanity's time on Earth, kids helped find, gather and prepare whole feasts of wild food because *all* food was wild. The same way you can spot your favorite brand of cookies from the far end of the grocery aisle, every family knew which berries to gobble up, and where to catch the best meat. These days, we still depend on nature for our food—we wouldn't have anything to eat without sun, rain and soil—but most of us find it easier to recognize a brand name than an edible native plant. Why? Like many stories, it started a long time ago, with some life-changing human inventions.

GROW IT YOURSELF

Humans have walked the Earth for about 200,000 years. For most of that time, all people followed their food. If delicious roots grew in the forest in spring, families were there to dig

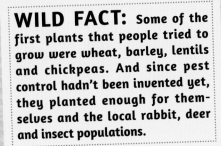

WILD FACT: Some of the first plants that people tried to grow were wheat, barley, lentils and chickpeas. And since pest control hadn't been invented yet, they planted enough for themselves and the local rabbit, deer and insect populations.

Blackberries! Yum! SHUTTERSTOCK.COM

8

Anyone hungry? These kids are catching small fish near a rice field on Bali, Indonesia. SHUTTERSTOCK.COM

them up. If antelope ran on the plains in summer, folks showed up to hunt. Then about 12,000 to 10,000 years ago, people in the Near East (the area from Iran to Egypt) tried to help nature along a bit. They cleared space around certain plants and watered them regularly. Those plants produced more food than wild ones, so some people stopped chasing their food and started growing it themselves. They had no idea that this shift would eventually make it possible for hundreds and even millions of people to live year-round in one place.

A WHEELY GOOD IDEA

For a few thousand years, farming families settled an area together and traded with *nomads* for foods and materials from other places. Meanwhile, travelers were coming up with new ways to haul goods. First they built sleds that their animals could drag along. And then, about 6,000 years ago, someone looked at a log and came up with a brilliant idea...wheels!

Growing food was so important to ancient Egyptians that they even put pictures of it on their tombs. WIKIMEDIA

Trees clean the air, protect the soil and shelter animals. They offered ancient people a zippier way to travel too. WIKIMEDIA

With wheels, suddenly everything was easier to carry, and once people created dirt roads between settlements, travel was faster than ever before. Settlements became larger, and while some people kept foraging or growing food, others began to specialize in one particular kind of job, like making shoes or building houses. Families traded with each other for skills or products that they needed.

With more and more people living in one place, local leaders had more work to do than ever before. Governments wrote and enforced laws, built and maintained roads and big buildings, and tried to keep life relatively peaceful for thousands of people. Cities were born.

NATURE? NOT TODAY, THANKS

The world's first cities developed just under 6,000 years ago, where Iraq is now. Within two thousand years, cities popped up in other places too—along the Nile Valley in Egypt, in the Indus Valley in present-day Pakistan, and along the Wei Valley in what's now China. Two thousand years ago, Mayan cities in what we know as Central America were going strong.

All cities were different, but around the world, city dwellers had at least one thing in common: the richer the family, the less contact they needed to have with nature. Being rich meant that someone else farmed for you or brought you the natural materials you needed or wanted. No need to rummage in the bush for your own breakfast anymore.

BEWARE THE WILD BEASTS!

Skip ahead from ancient times to medieval Europe, about 700 years ago. Country folk lived pretty much as they had for hundreds of years—growing their food, making most of their belongings and trading for anything else they needed. City life

WILD FACT: Ancient cities were home to humans, plants and animals alike. Trees offered shade, and livestock—like pigs, goats or chickens—often roamed the streets, eating garbage until the owners were ready to eat them. Trash-fed bacon, anyone?

was different. People lived extremely close together. When they needed something, they bought it. Garbage was a big problem. Most people just tossed theirs out the window, where rats feasted on it below. (Medieval cities must have been wonderful places to be a rat—plenty of food and no hawks, weasels or snakes to run away from!)

Meanwhile, traders continued to bring goods from city to city, as they had for thousands of years. But in 1347 they brought something else too: rats with fleas carrying a disease called the *bubonic plague.* These fleas jumped from rats to humans, enjoying fresh blood and spreading disease wherever they bit. Because people lived so close together and rats were everywhere, fleas had plenty of opportunity to jump onto a new rat or human host. Millions of people died, the disease never entirely disappeared, and 300 years later a huge outbreak happened all over again. In total, the bubonic plague killed about a fifth of the world's population.

Around the same time that city life was proving deadly in Europe, Europeans arrived in North America. They immediately

People still visit what's left of the ancient city of Mohenjo Daro in modern-day Pakistan. The city was built 4,500 years ago. WIKIMEDIA

Making Tracks

As a kid when I wasn't at school, at lessons or doing homework, my parents could find me at the creek. A long bark-mulch trail zigzagged down to the water, and I spent hours jumping from boulder to boulder, eating huckleberries, trying to catch tiny fish or building forts in overhanging trees.

This ravine between two subdivisions was my favorite playground as a kid.
MICHELLE MULDER

These Cree children lived at a residential school in 1945, but residential schools existed long after that. Canada didn't close its last one until 1996! BUD GLUNZ/NATIONAL FILM BOARD OF CANADA/LIBRARY AND ARCHIVES CANADA

noticed the close link that Indigenous peoples in North America had with nature. But instead of admiring how local people depended on and cared for nature so that it would continue to meet their needs, most European explorers called Native people "savages" and began loading local plants, rocks, animal parts and people (whom they kidnapped as slaves) onto their ships to bring home. Later, when Europeans moved to North America permanently, their new governments worked hard to stamp out the links that Indigenous people had with nature. In Canada, for example, for over 150 years, the government took Indigenous children away from their families and forced the kids to live in faraway schools. The idea was to make Indigenous children forget their own cultures and instead live like Canadians of European descent. (Governments around the world have run similar programs, with similarly disastrous results.) Imagine behaving that way and calling *other* people savage!

FACTORIES FOR THE FUTURE

Open a book about the history of cities, and you'll see drawings of buildings, statues and maybe even local celebrations. But it's a good thing those drawings aren't scratch-and-sniff because most cities around the world really stank! Garbage and poop (both animal and human) in the streets made city life a smelly adventure.

And in the 1700s, even more bad smells wafted up in many cities. In 1769, a Scottish man called James Watt invented the steam engine, and businessmen began using it to power machines for weaving and sewing. These machines could make clothing faster than people working by hand, and soon factories appeared all over Europe, puffing out smoke and dumping waste into local rivers and streams. Once the *Industrial Revolution* started, many plants and animals couldn't survive in cities anymore.

Blech! Who would want to breathe this city air?
WIKIMEDIA

Farm kids spent plenty of time outside. Those who moved to cities during the Industrial Revolution usually worked in factories.
LEWIS HINE/WIKIMEDIA

Early bicycles were so expensive that most kids never got to ride one unless they worked as messengers. WIKIMEDIA

This is what California's Highway 1 looked like in 1900. MARILYN GOULD/DREAMSTIME.COM

While pollution squeezed nature out, factory jobs brought more people in. For farmers who'd seen their crops rot or get eaten by insects, a factory job might have seemed like a dream come true. Working in a factory meant a guaranteed paycheck, no matter how wet the weather or how many insects were flying about.

Factories spewed out products faster than ever before, and to make those products they needed raw materials—wood chopped down in forests, metals dug out of the earth and water diverted from rivers. Nature had become a *resource* to be bought and sold.

PAVE IT!

Have you ever heard the expression *Don't reinvent the wheel?* It means *Use what you've got instead of creating something new.* But during the Industrial Revolution, *engineers* really did reinvent the wheel. With new knowledge about metals, and machines to do some very detailed work, engineers created one of the most efficient modes of transportation that has ever existed... the bicycle.

Europeans and North Americans loved bicycles. They were fast, and no one had to feed them, give them water or take them to the vet. People with bicycles could live farther away from their city jobs and still arrive at work on time. But the condition of the roads was a problem. Most of them were bumpy, and many were falling apart. In the United States in the late 1870s, cyclists began to *protest.* Eventually they convinced the American government that roads were important and should be paved and well-maintained.

This paved the way for another invention. In the early 1900s, automobiles became more and more common. With cars,

For early cyclists, this smooth road would have been a dream come true. This family is pedaling in Essen, Germany.
XAVIERARNAU/ISTOCK.COM

Making Tracks

In the late 1800s, bicycles were a super-speedy way to get around. Now cars and planes go much faster, but I prefer bicycle pace. When I explored Canada by bicycle, I was delighted to see moose peering at me from the bushes or eagles soaring above. I had time to talk with people I met, or to sit and watch birds in a campground or national park. I remember lots of details about my three-month pedaling experience and not a thing about the seven-hour plane trip home!

On my bike trip across Canada, trees provided shady picnic spots.
MICHELLE MULDER

15

people could work in the city, where most jobs were, but live in the countryside, where they could relax in their own piece of nature. Of course, that meant paving over a lot of natural areas to make the *commute* possible—and breaking up natural habitats into tiny, unconnected fragments—but more about that in the next chapter.

THROUGH THE CRACKS

Have you ever noticed that nature has a way of poking into our lives, even when we don't expect it? Grass grows up through a crack in the pavement. A tree root lifts the sidewalk. A snowstorm shuts the city down, or too much rain floods a basement. Around the world, many animals give up on living in the wild because city life is easier. Martens attack car engines in Dresden, Germany. Foxes hang out in London, England. Rattlesnakes slither through Phoenix, Arizona.

No matter how high we build our skyscrapers or how much pavement we lay down, we can't keep the natural world out of our cities (especially since, in many places, animals are running out of wild spaces to live in). We've tried with traps, *pesticides* and even with guns, but the natural habitat keeps creeping in, often in ways that scare us. Now many cities are trying a different approach. What if, instead of fighting wild nature off, we invite it in? What would city life look like *then*?

Kids who live near this tree on Vashon Island, Washington, know what happens when you leave your bike lying around. KENT PETERSON

CHAPTER TWO

Road Block

Wildlife grabbing a snack in Montreal, QC.
WIKIMEDIA

Is there food in here...or could it become a nest? Wild creatures in cities have to be adaptable.
FINWAL /ISTOCK.COM

HELLOOOO UNDER THERE!

What did your neighborhood look like before there were buildings? Was it a field of wild grasses? A forest? A desert? Chances are it was a thriving *ecosystem*—a community of tiny creatures, plants and animals. Some animals ate plants. Other animals ate the plant-eaters, and when any living being died, tiny *microorganisms* munched away, turning the dead matter into soil that fed the plants. Then the whole cycle started all over again.

This cycle still happens in cities, but with far fewer creatures involved. Some animals, like rats, gulls and squirrels, thrive between buildings full of humans. They feast on our garbage— or, if they're like coyotes, they feast on other animals that feast on our garbage—and they enjoy a rich life with few *predators*. The longer *urban* wildlife lives among people, the bolder animals become. Did you know that in Delhi, India, monkeys might swing down from rooftops to grab your lunch? Or that feral chickens in Miami, Florida, might flock in to eat your garden? Wild boars in Berlin, Germany, like nothing better than a quiet, dog-free backyard to birth their young.

While some creatures thrive in cities, most others disappear from the area. Frogs, for example, need to live near water because moist skin is crucial for their survival. When people build,

Some creatures survive better than others in cities. Half of India's 1.5-million monkeys are urban. Hang on to your lunch, folks!
DATYCH/DREAMSTIME.COM

though, the first task is to get rid of any water in the area. Frogs don't stand a chance in most cities. And no frogs means that the animals who eat them aren't likely to stick around either. Goodbye frogs, and goodbye snakes and many kinds of frog-eating birds too. A city ecosystem is very different from the one that was there before humans decided to build.

A LAWN? HOW ROYAL!

No doubt about it, the invention of cars changed the world. Those who could afford them covered great distances fast, making it possible to work downtown and live outside the city, surrounded by natural landscapes. But funnily enough, people who chose this lifestyle usually didn't want to live in a forest or in a grassland ecosystem with animals and insects. Instead, they wanted their land to look like that of other rich people, which meant destroying the local ecosystem and putting in lawn.

> **WILD FACT:** For the first time ever, most people in the world now live in cities. Our cities cover only 2 percent of Earth's surface, but they use up 75 percent of our planet's natural resources.

Planning to invade? Beware the lawn!
WIKIMEDIA

Would you believe the idea of lawns came from French castles 500 years ago? Back then, castle dwellers wanted to be able to spot invaders from a long way off, so they cut down the forests around their homes and let grass grow instead. Later, rich folk in England began growing lawns too, just to show how much money they had. (Only the rich could afford to pay someone to look after all that grass.) Europeans brought the idea to North America, and when the Industrial Revolution produced grass-cutting machines, suddenly everyone wanted a grassy yard.

Lawns can be made up of many kinds of grass, but chances are, most of them aren't native to the area. Native plants have spent thousands of years adapting to the weather in a certain region, but lawn grasses need humans to water them every summer. And when lawns get weedy, people often spray them with pesticides. (In some places, people even paint their grass green if it dries out!) Chemicals sprayed onto grass wind up in our soil and our water, and that's not good for any living creature. The ecosystems that were around before lawns not only looked after themselves, but they were better for everyone's health too.

BIODIVERSITY BLUES

In ecosystems, many different kinds of lifeforms live together, from bacteria to plants to big meat-eaters. Each species has evolved over thousands of years to perform a very specific job (usually eating another creature to keep it from taking over), and this variety of life in an ecosystem is called *biodiversity.* But often newcomers or *introduced species* arrive. Maybe a plant seed travels secretly on a person's muddy boot, or perhaps someone brings a new plant or animal into an ecosystem on purpose. Introduced species can cause plenty of problems. The grass we plant for lawns is an introduced species, for example. Few native species have evolved to feast on it, so many local creatures have to go elsewhere to find food. Other introduced species, like English ivy, aren't only jobless, they're harmful—they actually choke out native species and replace them. *Help!* Beware of the invasive plants!

Tired of guzzling gas with a modern mower? In many North American cities, people can rent goats to keep their grass trimmed and fertilized.
DREAMSTIME.COM

Making Tracks

My daughter's favorite part of our local playground is the wooded area around it—with a bushy area to build forts in, trees to climb and plenty of food! Happily, our city does not spray with pesticides, and in June my daughter and I love picking salmonberries. Then come thimbleberries and later blackberries. Lately we've been learning about other native plants we can eat, and now we wander through town munching on miner's lettuce, honesty flowers and the occasional dandelion. (I even made dandelion pancakes once, but those tasted like, well, grass.)

Free snacks at the local playground! GASTÓN CASTAÑO

Pedaling through flooded Calgary, AB. DREAMSTIME.COM

A resident looks on as the Elbow River overflows its banks in Calgary. ISTOCK.COM

MAKE WAY FOR WATER

Plants. They feed us, and they clean the air. But did you know that they help keep water out of our basements too?

Water has been traveling around our planet for billions of years, falling from the sky, soaking into the ground, freezing into ice, mixing with the ocean, getting slurped up by thirsty creatures, or evaporating back into the sky where it becomes rain and snow again. But the *water cycle* depends on soft ground for the water to soak into the earth. Have you ever seen water soak into asphalt or concrete? It can't. In fact, water won't even soak into dirt that has dried hard. Instead, it rolls along the top until it reaches a dip in the ground, like an underground parkade, a subway tunnel or a basement.

In 2013, huge parts of Calgary, Alberta, flooded. The city's solution? First, clean up the mess, and then tear up the pavement (or some of it, anyway). An organization called Depave Paradise

At Brooklands School in Winnipeg, MB, students and community members transformed an unused basketball court into a beautiful outdoor classroom...in just one day! ERIN CLARKE

works in communities across the country to rip out pavement and plant native plants instead. Soon the plants attract native insects. Those insects attract small birds, who in turn attract small animals back to that area of the city. *Ta da!* From flooding hazard to wildlife refuge!

REWILD THE WILDLIFE!

If making homes for wildflowers is good for an ecosystem, should we make supper for wildlife too?

Actually, wildlife experts agree that feeding wild creatures—even birds—is a dangerous idea. The more animals rely on humans for food, the less able they'll be to look after themselves.

WILD FACT: Around 1890, Eugene Schieffelin released 100 European starlings in New York City, as a gift to the local people. These first starlings in North America soon spread across the continent, destroying the eggs of native birds and taking over their nests. These days, the United States is home to 200 million starlings (and fewer native species than before).

This is for the birds! (But how many other creatures might eat the seeds instead?) ISTOCK.COM

In bear country, an unlocked garbage can is like sending local wildlife a dinner invitation. ISTOCK.COM

(Besides, sometimes the food we offer isn't even eaten by the animal we intend to feed. In the United States, people spend $2.7 billion on birdseed every year, and rats, squirrels and even bears often munch on the seed instead!)

For years now, folks in England have watched wild foxes explore backyards and city gardens. Some people have offered food, and many foxes have become accustomed to humans…so accustomed, in fact, that they'll often march right into houses, looking for a handout. Instead of building dens in the soil, many foxes move into people's basements. These changes aren't good for foxes (who become less and less able to survive in the wild) or for humans (because foxes are still wild animals, unpredictable and sometimes carrying diseases). Living close to nature is a good thing, but only if nature doesn't get too used to us.

Folks in the small mountain town of Banff, Alberta, found this out the hard way. In the 1960s, Parks Canada tried to protect local humans by killing wolves and many of the cougars in the area. Boy, did that make the elk happy! With none of their usual predators around, elk thrived in record numbers. Soon they ate all the willow trees, which wiped out the local beaver population. In the 1980s, park officials realized that getting rid of wolves and cougars wasn't a great plan after all, so they stopped killing them. With more predators in the forest, the elk moved into town. The big, beautiful creatures munched on gardens and blocked streets, and people gave them space. But then the grizzly bears started to arrive, looking for elk meat. Locals had to make a choice—live with the constant threat of grizzlies roaming the streets, or scare away the elk. For safety, people chose the second option.

Scientists point out that the best way to protect wild creatures is to protect their natural food sources and to keep them wild—in other words, wary of humans and fully capable of fending for themselves.

In some neighborhoods, nature can be hard to find. These kids are enjoying time outside in Mardin, Turkey.
TEKINTURKDOGAN /ISTOCK.COM

Making Tracks

Okay. I'll admit it. Much as I love our apartment building, I wish we had a yard with climbing trees and a pond. Instead, we've found other ways to include nature in our lives. We go to the beach and local parks, we built garden boxes in our parking spot (we don't own a car), we've grown edible mushrooms on a log in our bathroom, and we keep worms in our closet. Yes, worms! Our *vermicomposter* worms chew up most of our vegetable scraps and give us rich soil for our plants. They also make a great conversation topic when friends come for supper!

Please feed the worms! MICHELLE MULDER

25

Humans love London, England, for the history and the culture. Foxes love it for all the food and the lack of predators! ISTOCK.COM

SPROUTING SOMETHING GOOD

It's a fine balance. Cities without nature can be hot, stinky and unpleasant. Let too much nature in, though, and you've got grizzlies in the streets, foxes in the basement or wild boars in the backyard. *Eek!*

Even though we don't want big, wild animals making themselves at home in our living rooms, biodiversity is still important in cities. Why? Because no matter how much our cities usually separate us from the rest of nature, we humans are still part of the natural world. We rely on it for food and water, fuel to keep us warm, fibers to make clothing, and even the mineral *coltan* for making cell phones. Our every action affects the rest of nature too, and in the last few centuries we've had a bigger impact on our planet than ever before. Ever-increasing human activity is leaving other creatures with less and less wild space. Cities in particular have become so dense, polluted and noisy that most other species can't survive in them. The species that *can* survive have few predators, which means that sometimes rats and cockroaches seem to be taking over the world. For all these reasons, more and more cities want to shift the balance and invite nature back in.

But how? If you're living in a high-rise, and the only dirt in your life is the grime of car exhaust, rewilding our cities might seem impossible. But it doesn't have to be. Rewilding can be as complex as depaving a creek or as simple as planting a few seeds. All you need is a bit of time, curiosity, keen eyes and creativity. You'll be working alongside people around the world who are rewilding too, and your actions won't just change cities. They can save species, improve human health and make the world a safer place for everyone. Wild city life, here we come!

Hoping for a greener city? Why not help grow it yourself? ISTOCK.COM

On the ground or on the roof, trees can be home to many different species. These trees are growing in Monte Carlo, Monaco.
ISTOCK.COM

CHAPTER THREE

Life in the City

Not long ago, this part of Seoul, South Korea, was a busy highway. When the city depaved, Cheonggyecheon Stream came alive again.
IMKENNETH/DREAMSTIME.COM

The stream Cheonggyecheon in Seoul, South Korea, isn't very wild in some parts, but it's still home to many wild creatures.
ISTOCK.COM

MY WAY OR THE HIGHWAY?

If you were an *urban planner,* what would you put in the middle of your city: a highway or a park? In 2003, Seoul, South Korea, chose to get rid of a downtown highway to restore what had been there before: a burbling, meandering stream.

With great excitement, city workers bashed apart the pavement that had covered the stream for almost fifty years, and underneath they found...barely a trickle of water. *No problem*, said the local government, and they gave orders to pump 120,000 tons of water from other local streams, a river, and even from below subway stations. Soon the stream was home to fish, insects and birds alike. Seoul opened it to the public in 2005, and families and friends have been picnicking there ever since. Goodbye highway, hello thriving ecosystem in the middle of a bustling city.

MARSH THIS WAY

In many cities the landscape is constantly changing. For example, big parts of East London, England, used to be polluted industrial areas. And long before that they were *wetlands*

Imagine getting back to the wilderness, right in your neighborhood. This family is in Woodberry Wetlands in London, England. ALAMY STOCK PHOTO

(marshes) whose special blend of plants, rocks and silt worked together to clean countless liters of water every year.

These days, East London wants its wetlands back. In 2014, workers began to refill the marsh, plant reeds, and release ducks and other waterfowl into the area. By 2017, the marshes of East London made up Europe's largest urban wetland. Imagine an industrial wasteland at the end of your street suddenly becoming a lush haven for wildlife. Forget homework. Let's go fishing!

GOING WILD DOWNTOWN

A few years ago, a deer walked into a toy store in downtown Victoria, British Columbia. It sounds like the beginning of a joke, but it's really true. The funny part is that at first the shopkeepers didn't notice because the animal blended in with the plush toys for sale!

WILD FACT: New York City is home to millions of rats— plenty of food for the coyotes and foxes that live in Central Park. In fact, some New Yorkers would like to see more coyotes in the park, simply to help control the rat population!

Hmm. Now where was that crosswalk again?
ISTOCK.COM

Deer are common in quieter parts of Victoria, where they have no natural predators and they feast on people's gardens, but they rarely venture downtown. Like most wild creatures, they prefer to stay in green areas with lots of food and without much car traffic. In Victoria, as in most cities, such places are so far apart that animals rarely risk the journey from one to another.

But what if wildlife could travel throughout a city without fear of being seen or run over? That was the idea in Helsinki, Finland, where planners developed "green fingers," or long connected areas of wilderness that stretch from downtown to the city limits. The concept worked so well that wildlife can now travel from one end to another without encountering a car or even a human. Finding a mate and a delicious supper is easier for animals now because they can roam far and wide instead of living in broken-up bits of wild ecosystem. Rats and pigeons aren't the only creatures you might see in the city anymore. Now you can spot badgers, arctic hare and elk right in the middle of Helsinki.

Making Tracks

My husband is from Buenos Aires, Argentina, a big South American city. Highways run over, through and around the city. Some cars are the latest models, and others are so old that the doors are tied on with rope. On my first visit, I noticed several families pulling off the highway onto small patches of grass near the exits. At first I assumed that their cars had broken down, but when they lifted baskets of food from their trunks, I realized that the tiny, noisy, smoggy, green spaces had become picnic destinations!

Enough green space for a picnic?
ISTOCK.COM

BIG, SCARY NATURE

Wait a minute! Wait a minute! Depaving, planting native species, creating more wild spaces in cities—will cities even *be* cities anymore?

It's true that as we clean up the wild spaces in our cities (like lakes and rivers) and make room for more wildness (in flowerpots on balconies or in depaved schoolyards), more creatures will be able to enjoy city life, but that doesn't mean that wildlife will crowd out the humans. Most wild animals don't trust us and would rather avoid humans. In fact, many cities, like Chicago, Illinois, are already home to large numbers of big *carnivores* like coyotes, but they're so good at hiding that people rarely see them. Besides, most wildlife officials suggest that we should be more scared of *people* than urban wildlife—speeding cars or distracted drivers kill far more humans than wild animals ever do!

Coyotes are not picky eaters, and city life offers them a long menu, from insects to rodents to garbage. NORTHOHANA/ISTOCK.COM

THE HOST WITH THE MOST

Luckily, you don't have to wait for adults to tear up a highway or refill a marsh to create new ecosystems in your neighborhood. In Adelaide, Australia, kids from 180 schools helped plant three million native trees throughout the city. It took eleven years, and now the trees help clean the air, lower city temperatures and provide homes for local wildlife. And we're not just talking about a few birds and insects. Trees that are native to an area can attract hundreds of different species.

In Baltimore County, Maryland, local foresters used to plant ginkgo trees along the streets. Originally from China, these trees grow well in cities around the world. But scientists pointed out that only three local species can make their homes in a ginkgo tree, and the oak trees native to Baltimore can host 537! So now new laws insist that at least half of all trees planted

Ginkgos are common in cities, but many species avoid them...and that includes humans. In autumn, ginkgo fruit smells like dog poop. Blech! ISTOCK.COM

in the county be native oaks, and species from caterpillars to songbirds are thriving. Even fish (which eat creatures that feed on oak leaves at the bottom of streambeds) are enjoying this new biodiversity bonanza.

FLOWER POWER

Not up for planting three million trees? What about a handful of seeds? A single patch of native wildflowers on a balcony, in a yard or even in an empty lot can attract insects from mason bees to butterflies.

Native plants are a crucial part of the ecosystem, and many creatures, including *pollinators* like bees, depend on them. Pollinators travel from plant to plant, collecting nectar, and in the process they spread pollen from one plant to another. This pollen mix-up is how plants reproduce, make many of the fruits and vegetables that humans eat, and keep feeding the other creatures

How many wild creatures will this new flower feed? ERICA BIRD

Imagine how flower filled cities would be if they all had community seed stations like this one.

IMAGE COURTESY OF THE ALBRIGHT-KNOX ART GALLERY DIGITAL ASSETS COLLECTION. PHOTOGRAPH BY TOM LOONAN.

of the world too. But these days, in many parts of the world, pollinator numbers are declining. Europe has created new laws that ban certain pesticides and *genetically modified* plants, which harm pollinators, and already European pollinators are growing in numbers. Meanwhile, in cities around the globe, people are planting native wildflower gardens to attract and feed pollinators. These splashes of color can really perk up a *concrete jungle.*

And that's part of the idea behind artist Jenny Kendler's project *ReWilding New York: Community Seed Stations.* With the help of the Albright-Knox Art Gallery in Buffalo, New York, Jenny placed colorful, *upcycled* newspaper boxes all over western New York state. If you wandered down a street in Buffalo in 2015, you might have noticed one with a small flower garden on top. Open the door in the front, and you'd find packets of wildflower seeds, free for the taking. You could plant them wherever you liked, help save monarch butterflies from extinction and bring a city into bloom. Now imagine

Many people don't want clover—or any other native plants—in their lawns, but bees love the little flowers. ISTOCK.COM

33

A bit of wood, some nails and a hammer are all it takes to build a bat house. Mosquitoes, watch out! DREAMSTIME.COM

9,999 other people doing the same, and picture how beautiful summertime would be!

GOING BATTY

If flowers aren't your thing, what about bats? By putting up a bat house, you could be doing your part to save an entire species. And the bats will thank you for it in a delightful way. Did you know that a single bat eats up to 1,000 mosquitoes in an hour?

Bat houses—and birdhouses and even houses for mason bees—are what's known as *habitecture,* human-made structures built to house wild creatures. For thousands of years, houses in England have included dovecotes in the outside walls, creating homes for pigeons. Local farmers collected the pigeon poop for fertilizer, and some people even used pigeons to send messages to friends long before email or even telephones were invented. In Poland, people used to put carriage wheels on top of their houses for storks to nest on. And folks around the world enjoy having "bee boles" (tiny homes for bees) built into their exterior walls. The rent paid by honeybees is delicious!

Habitecture isn't always intentional though. For instance, in Austin, Texas, more than a million Mexican free-tailed bats make their home in the Congress Avenue Bridge. In the early 1980s, the city considered killing the bats, but Bat Conservation International kicked up a fuss, and now Austin is the proud home of the world's largest urban bat colony. In the summer, crowds of tourists gather at sunset to watch a million winged creatures zoom out of the bridge for their nighttime hunt. (And experienced tourists know to bring an umbrella if they want to go home clean.)

THE DIRT ON CITIES

Have you ever noticed that it's easier to slow down in a forest or walking along a beach? For many people, city life means

This bee box in a community garden in Victoria, BC, welcomes native bees to nest...and encourages local humans to learn about pollinators. ELLA COLLIER

living *fast*—zooming from one place to another in a car or a subway, bustling along sidewalks, or hurrying to do the last bit of shopping before the store closes. When we wander in wild spaces, we rarely need to hurry. It's all about relaxing into our surroundings. In fact, natural settings like forests or beaches are proven to lower human stress levels and help prevent all sorts of health problems, from *obesity* to mental illness. In the United States, the National Recreation and Park Association is partnering with the Centers for Disease Control and Prevention to get more doctors to prescribe…time in parks! When cities include wild spaces, locals enjoy nature, not as a bunch of resources to buy and sell, but as our home. We're all part of it.

Want to find more wildness in your own neighborhood? How about creating a few new wild spaces yourself? Time to head outside!

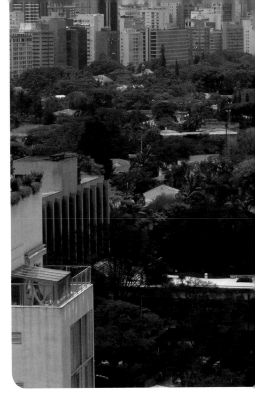

Plenty of trees make the Jardins neighborhood in São Paulo, Brazil, a cool place to live.
WIKIMEDIA

Making Tracks

Last fall, a cougar ran through a Victoria neighborhood. After a dramatic chase with sirens blaring, crows squawking and dozens of humans looking on, *conservation officers* tranquilized and relocated the animal to a forest far from the city. For days, everyone seemed to be talking about our brush with danger, and I wondered if maybe rewilding cities isn't such a good idea after all. (Making space for wild nature like cougars? Aack!) But cougars are shy creatures that generally stay out of sight. If we give them more space to do that, they're less likely to show up in our yards.

Beautiful but scary in the backyard. SHUTTERSTOCK.COM

CHAPTER FOUR

Wildlife Welcome

CLIMB THAT TREE!

What's less risky, climbing a tree or watching TV? The answer might surprise you! Health organizations around the world note that many kids spend all their time indoors—in school, at home or in a car. And more kids than ever struggle with obesity and related problems because they don't get enough exercise. That's why, these days, doctors say the biggest risk for kids *isn't* outdoor play. It's staying inside!

SIDEWALK SAFARI

But what if your neighborhood doesn't have any trees to climb in? What if there's no nature anywhere?

Impossible! And you can prove it. Just grab a sun hat (or rain boots) and head outdoors. Time to go on a sidewalk safari. Weed-filled empty lots or grassy patches are great places to start, but even a tiny weed poking up through the pavement will do. Take a close look. Do you see any insects on it? If so, then you've discovered an important part of the local food chain. (Plants feed insects, which attract bigger animals like birds, who in turn attract other creatures. In time, you'll be

Unlike monkey bars, growing trees offer a new challenge each time you climb...fun for both bodies and brains. ISTOCK.COM

Traditional playgrounds are made of painted metal. Nature playgrounds use wood, rocks and even plants. This one's in London, England and is designed by Erect Architecture. DAVID GRANDORGE

able to help this process along in patches throughout your neighborhood.) Once you've spotted an interesting plant or animal, look up your fellow creature online or at a library. If you're new to nature-watching, you'll soon find a whole world of fascinating creatures right outside your door.

DIRT TO THE RESCUE

Plants and animals aren't the only creatures humans need in cities. We also need microscopic creatures called microbes or microorganisms. Did you know that every one of us is home to 100 trillion microbes? In our guts alone, we host 500 to 1,000 different microbe species.

WILD FACT: It's official. In 2015, at an international conference in Helsinki, Finland, scientists announced that playing outside is crucial for good health.

Some of our helpful microorganisms come from the food we eat, and other handy microbes come from our environment. For example, one little critter called *Mycobacterium vaccae* is found in wet soil and is known to help people fight anxiety and depression. In fact, studies show that sticking your hands in the dirt can help build immunity to diseases, improve mood and even help heart function. Of course, it's always a good idea to wash hands regularly, because not all microbes are good for our health, but *some* microbes are very good for us indeed. If we're stuck inside all the time, or there's no dirt to get our hands into, then it's harder to get in touch with these helpful little critters.

Can some of the invisible creatures in soil help fight depression? You bet! ISTOCK.COM

FIND YOUR HUMAN HERD

What if going to school meant spending each day…in a forest? Every morning, students at "forest schools" in Copenhagen, Denmark, get on buses to wilderness areas and spend their days learning about nature. But even if your school is firmly planted in the city, you can still spend time in nature with other kids and adults.

Each year, more cities offer nature clubs. In Toronto, Ontario, kids can join a local after-school program run by an organization called the p.i.n.e. project. Kids learn how to identify and gather wild foods, how to recognize animal tracks, how to light a fire in all kinds of weather, and how to survive in the wilderness.

Other kids help create wild spaces in their own schoolyards. Kids at Dundas Central Public School in Dundas, Ontario, worked with teachers and parents to rewild. Together, they ripped up pavement and planted an interpretive wetland and a woodland garden right outside their classrooms. Now many of their classes are held outdoors, calculating how much water a wetland can clean, or learning about the creatures that live there. Imagine what could happen with the paved areas at your school!

Thriving Roots Wilderness School teaches kids on Vancouver Island how to survive—and thrive—in nature. ALAINA HALLETT

TREE-MENDOUS KID POWER

Can kids stop tsunamis and hurricanes from flooding a city? Yes!

Adeline Tiffanie Suwana grew up in Indonesia. The capital city, Jakarta, often flooded because hard rains simply rolled off bare soil and pooled in the city. In 2008, ten-year-old Adeline decided to do something about it. During a school holiday, she invited almost 150 young friends to plant mangrove trees. The trees keep the soil from washing away and help the ground suck up water. Together, they protect an entire city from tsunami and hurricane damage. And Adeline and her friends haven't stopped there. They've formed an organization in Indonesia called *Sahabat Alam* (Friends of Nature). The group has planted coral reefs to replace the damaged ones surrounding the island, they've helped with fish breeding and turtle protection, and they've presented their ideas to schools and government agencies. Kid power really can change the world!

> **WILD FACT:** January in Yellowknife, NWT, is dark and cold, and schools keep kids inside for recess when the temperature falls below -30° Celsius (-22° Fahrenheit). But in 2013, many students wrote to their school district to protest. Even at -39° Celsius (-38.2° Fahrenheit) they wanted an outdoor recess, because in January it's the only chance they get to see the sun!

BE A SCIENTIST, CITIZEN

Did you know that scientists often rely on kids like you to make major discoveries? Scientists like to learn as much as they can about their favorite subject, but since they can't be in all places at all times, they often rely on other people to be their eyes and ears. They want to know about nature in your neighborhood, and thanks to the Internet, it's easy to join citizen scientist projects. Would you like to learn about frog calls? Or how owls fly? What about studying worms in the Great Lakes, or what ladybugs like to eat? Whatever your interest, there's likely a citizen science project that could use your help.

In citizen science, being a kid is a huge advantage. For one thing, young people see the world from a different height, which means you often spot things that a taller person might miss. And in general, kids are better at noticing the world around us.

People can thrive outdoors even at -39° Celsius (-38.2° Fahrenheit). These kids are at a Dene cultural winter camp near Yellowknife in northern Canada. BOBBY DRYGEESE

While adults are often distracted by phones, conversations or even our own thoughts, kids hear bird calls, watch the swoop of a swallowtail butterfly or smell the rain that's about to arrive. Interested in putting all those skills to good use? Check out the resources at the end of this book to find science projects that need your help.

WALKING ON THE WILD SIDE

Have you ever seen those TV shows where people compete against each other to survive in nature? With wild animals jumping out from behind trees, poisonous berries tempting the hungry and not a single grocery store in sight, nature is the enemy, threatening at every turn.

But that's only because most of us haven't grown up in nature like our ancestors did. How often do we learn how to harvest wild food, find clean water or build a shelter these days? Everything we need in daily life comes from nature at some

This forest is a classroom for students at Saturna Ecological Education Centre, a public school in southwestern BC. CHRISTOPHER KING

Making Tracks

My dad's not a big fan of dirt. He doesn't like it on his clothes or his shoes, and certainly not on his hands. So when he sees my daughter playing in the mud, up to her arms in it, he shakes his head sadly. A few weeks ago, I overheard my daughter reassuring him with something I'd learned while researching this book. "Don't worry. It's part of nature, and getting my hands in the dirt is good for my immunity." She even offered to spread some mud on his arm but, strangely, he didn't take her up on it!

Who needs toys when you've got mud?
MICHELLE MULDER

What if your school day involved splashing around in tide pools, poking at sea anemones, sampling blackberries and exploring ant hills? JOHN RUSSELL

point, yet nature itself doesn't feel like home anymore. In other words, we humans are totally dependent on the health of the natural world, yet we're often scared to be in it!

Kids around the world are working together to change all that. Some kids spend every summer camping, getting to know local plants and animals in their area. Other young people go to wilderness schools where they learn to fish, forage, track animals and build shelters out of grass and sticks. (And some of these schools can even be found in the middle of huge cities, like New York!)

You don't need to go *anywhere* to rewild your life and your neighborhood though. Here's how you can get started right now, right where you are.

Raining? No problem! Tree cover and good rain gear keep students dry on a wet day.
CHRISTOPHER KING

Find It!

Most cities are home to nature clubs. You might even find one at your school. But if you can't find a nature-loving human herd anywhere, you can always gather a bunch of friends and ask a knowledgeable adult to introduce you to nearby native plants and animals. Get ready to discover fascinating new neighbors in your 'hood!

Plant It!

A handful of seeds can go a long way, and you don't need much space to invite native insects and other animals into your area. A pot on a balcony, or even a crack in the sidewalk, can make a perfect spot for a little native garden.

A keen eye can unearth some fascinating wild neighbors you never knew you had!
JOHN RUSSELL

These wriggling superheroes produce the soil that feeds the plants that feed the world.
SHUTTERSTOCK.COM

Saving the planet, one hilarious ride at a time.
ISTOCK.COM

Green It!

If given half a chance, nature knows exactly what to do with an empty lot or a patch of bare ground. Why not adopt a bit of earth in your area and help keep it clear from litter? Then stand back and watch as a vibrant ecosystem sprouts up before you.

Compost It!

Nature can be just as enjoyable inside as outdoors. A vermicomposter under your kitchen sink is a great way to keep vegetable scraps out of the landfill (where they produce harmful gases) and turn them into soil instead. And what better way to learn about one of the most important parts of any ecosystem—soil. Plants can't live without it, and the rest of us can't live without plants, so soil is powerful stuff.

Rethink It!

Did you know that every time you decide against buying something, you're giving nature a helping hand? The less we buy, the fewer resources (bits of nature) we use up. Using fewer resources includes using less gasoline or diesel. Every time you walk or pedal your way somewhere, you're looking after our home (and your body too). Many people, all deciding to buy less, can save entire habitats from being destroyed.

WELCOME HOME

Our planet is home to thousands of cities, and for the first time ever, most humans are now city dwellers. But that doesn't mean we need to live separated from the rest of nature.

Wilder cities are proving both safer and more enjoyable places to live—for humans and wildlife alike. Humans need nature, and together we can make sure that life on our planet thrives, not just far away on distant hilltops, but right here in our cities too.

No matter where you live, wild nature offers a lifetime of possibilities to explore. CHRISTOPHER KING

Resources

Print

Burns, Loree Griffin. *Citizen Scientists: Be a Part of Scientific Discovery from Your Own Backyard.* New York: Henry Holt & Co., 2012.

Leslie, Clare Walker. *The Nature Connection: An Outdoor Workbook for Kids, Families, and Classrooms.* North Adams, MA: Storey Publishing, 2010.

Mason, Adrienne. *Planet Ark: Preserving Earth's Biodiversity.* Toronto: Kids Can Press, 2013.

Read, Nicholas. *City Critters: Wildlife in the Urban Jungle.* Victoria: Orca Book Publishers, 2012.

Wilcox, Merrie-Ellen. *What's the Buzz? Keeping Bees in Flight.* Victoria: Orca Book Publishers, 2015.

Online

Roots & Shoots (International Wildlife Conservation for Youth): www.rootsandshoots.org

SciStarter (Citizen Science): www.scistarter.com

World Wildlife Fund: www.worldwildlife.org

Acknowledgments

I love the acknowledgments section. It's where I get to celebrate the incredible team that put this book together. Thank you, Chris Adams, for gifting me the book idea and for helping with the proposal. Thank you, too, Susannah. Many thanks to Canada Council for the Arts for the generous financial support that allowed me to work on this project. I'm grateful to Steve Duncan and Susan and Gary Braley for help with photos. Thank you, David Krieger and Adam Bienenstock, for sharing your experience with a random writer who called out of the blue. Your inspiring stories helped reshape my entire worldview. I'm grateful to all the talented, dedicated and endlessly creative folks at Orca who turned my words into a beautiful book. And thanks to my husband, Gastón (who has joined me on crazy, mapless escapades from Salt Spring Island to Lago Titicaca), and to Maia (who gets her boots on faster than I can say "outdoor adventure" each time I want to go outside). And, of course, thank you to everyone who loves, enjoys and protects the wildness in the world. What an amazing planet we all get to enjoy!

Glossary

biodiversity—the variety of species found in a particular ecosystem

bubonic plague—bacterial infection outbreaks in the 1300s and 1600s that killed about one fifth of the world's human population

carnivore—any creature that eats meat

coltan—a dull black metallic ore used in the production of cell phones and other electronics

commute—a regular journey to and from one's place of work

concrete jungle—an expression to describe a place made mostly of concrete or similar materials, especially one that lacks plants

conservation officer—law enforcers who are responsible for protecting the environment and making sure that an area's natural resources are used wisely and responsibly

ecosystem—a complex system in which everything that exists in a particular environment relies on the other parts of that environment in some way

engineer—a designer or builder of materials, structures and systems

feral—an animal or plant that has not been domesticated or cultivated

genetically modified—a plant, animal, or other life form that is different from its ancestors because humans have changed its genes (parts of the cells that control the living thing's appearance and growth)

global warming—a gradual increase in the average temperature of the Earth's atmosphere and its oceans, which is believed to be permanently changing the Earth's climate

habitecture—human-made structures built to house wild creatures

Industrial Revolution—the shift to new manufacturing processes where machines made products that people had always made by hand; the shift took place from 1760 to sometime between 1820 and 1840

introduced species—plants or animals, brought in from somewhere else, that can crowd out the plants and animals that are native to a place

microorganism—an organism too small to see without a microscope, especially a bacterium, virus or fungus

native—plants or animals living or growing naturally in a particular region

nomad—a member of a community of people who live in different locations, moving from one place to another

obesity—a condition where a person has so much body fat that it might have a negative effect on their health

pesticide—a poison that is used to kill insects and weeds

pollinator—an insect or other animal that carries pollen from one plant to another

predator—an animal that naturally preys on others

protest—a statement or action showing that people disapprove of or object to something

resource—material, energy, service, staff or knowledge used to make a product

rewilding—to return the land to its natural state, full of local native species

upcycling—the process of transforming waste materials, useless or unwanted products into new materials or products; also known as creative reuse

urban—relating to cities

urban planner—someone who develops plans and programs for the use of land in towns, cities and metropolitan areas

vermicomposter—a bin where various species of worms recycle vegetable scraps into compost

water cycle—the natural process of water changing from vapor in the air to rain or snow, then landing on Earth's surface, and eventually evaporating back into the air

wetlands—areas of land whose special blend of plants, rocks and silt work together to clean countless liters of water every year

Index

Index (continued)